Love

R. S.

A Phoenix Paperback

The Collected Poems by R. S. Thomas first published
by J. M. Dent in 1993

This abridged edition published in 1996 by Phoenix
a division of Orion Books Ltd
Orion House, 5 Upper St Martin's Lane, London WC2H 9EA

Copyright © 1993, 1996 R. S. Thomas

Cover illustration:
'The Pond at Charleston', by Duncan Grant, Christie's Images

ISBN 1 85799 677 1

Typeset by Selwood Systems, Midsomer Norton, Avon
Printed in Great Britain by Clays Ltd, St Ives plc

CONTENTS

The Hill Farmer Speaks

I am the farmer, stripped of love
And thought and grace by the land's hardness;
But what I am saying over the fields'
Desolate acres, rough with dew,
Is, Listen, listen, I am a man like you.

The wind goes over the hill pastures
Year after year, and the ewes starve,
Milkless, for want of the new grass.
And I starve, too, for something the spring
Can never foster in veins run dry.

The pig is a friend, the cattle's breath
Mingles with mine in the still lanes;
I wear it willingly like a cloak
To shelter me from your curious gaze.

The hens go in and out at the door
From sun to shadow, as stray thoughts pass
Over the floor of my wide skull.
The dirt is under my cracked nails;
The tale of my life is smirched with dung;
The phlegm rattles. But what I am saying
Over the grasses rough with dew
Is, Listen, listen, I am a man like you.

The Unborn Daughter

On her unborn in the vast circle
Concentric with our finite lives;
On her unborn, her name uncurling
Like a young fern within the mind;
On her unclothed with flesh or beauty
In the womb's darkness, I bestow
The formal influence of the will,
The wayward influence of the heart,
Weaving upon her fluid bones
The subtle fabric of her being,
Hair, hands and eyes, the body's texture,
Shot with the glory of the soul.

Song at the Year's Turning

Shelley dreamed it. Now the dream decays.
The props crumble. The familiar ways
Are stale with tears trodden underfoot.
The heart's flower withers at the root.
Bury it, then, in history's sterile dust.
The slow years shall tame your tawny lust.

Love deceived him; what is there to say
The mind brought you by a better way
To this despair? Lost in the world's wood
You cannot stanch the bright menstrual blood.
The earth sickens; under naked boughs
The frost comes to barb your broken vows.

Is there blessing? Light's peculiar grace
In cold splendour robes this tortured place
For strange marriage. Voices in the wind
Weave a garland where a mortal sinned.
Winter rots you; who is there to blame?
The new grass shall purge you in its flame.

In a Country Church

To one kneeling down no word came,
Only the wind's song, saddening the lips
Of the grave saints, rigid in glass;
Or the dry whisper of unseen wings,
Bats not angels, in the high roof.

Was he balked by silence? He kneeled long,
And saw love in a dark crown
Of thorns blazing, and a winter tree
Golden with fruit of a man's body.

Chapel Deacon

Who put that crease in your soul,
Davies, ready this fine morning
For the staid chapel, where the Book's frown
Sobers the sunlight ? Who taught you to pray
And scheme at once, your eyes turning
Skyward, while your swift mind weighs
Your heifer's chances in the next town's
Fair on Thursday ? Are your heart's coals
Kindled for God, or is the burning
Of your lean cheeks because you sit
Too near that girl's smouldering gaze ?
Tell me, Davies, for the faint breeze
From heaven freshens and I roll in it,
Who taught you your deft poise ?

Age

Farmer, you were young once.
And she was there, waiting, the unique flower
That only you could find in the wild moor
Of your experience.
Gathered, she grew to the warm woman
Your hands had imagined
Fondling soil in the spring fields.

And she was fertile; four strong sons
Stood up like corn in June about you.
But, farmer, did you cherish, tend her
As your own flesh, this dry stalk
Where the past murmurs its sad tune?
Is this the harvest of your blithe sowing?

If you had spared from your long store
Of days lavished upon the land
But one for her where she lay fallow,
Drying, hardening, withering to waste.
But now – too late! You're an old tree,
Your roots groping in her in vain.

Ap Huw's Testament

There are four verses to put down
For the four people in my life,
Father, mother, wife

And the one child. Let me begin
With her of the immaculate brow
My wife ; she loves me. I know how.

My mother gave me the breast's milk
Generously, but grew mean after,
Envying me my detached laughter.

My father was a passionate man,
Wrecked after leaving the sea
In her love's shallows. He grieves in me.

What shall I say of my boy,
Tall, fair? He is young yet ;
Keep his feet free of the world's net.

Bread

Hunger was loneliness, betrayed
By the pitiless candour of the stars'
Talk, in an old byre he prayed

Not for food; to pray was to know
Waking from a dark dream to find
The white loaf on the white snow;

Not for warmth, warmth brought the rain's
Blurring of the essential point
Of ice probing his raw pain.

He prayed for love, love that would share
His rags' secret; rising he broke
Like sun crumbling the gold air

The live bread for the starved folk.

Farm Wife

Hers is the clean apron, good for fire
Or lamp to embroider, as we talk slowly
In the long kitchen, while the white dough
Turns to pastry in the great oven,
Sweetly and surely as hay making
In a June meadow; hers are the hands,
Humble with milking, but still now
In her wide lap as though they heard
A quiet music, hers being the voice
That coaxes time back to the shadows
In the room's corners. O, hers is all
This strong body, the safe island
Where men may come, sons and lovers,
Daring the cold seas of her eyes.

Anniversary

Nineteen years now
Under the same roof
Eating our bread,
Using the same air;
Sighing, if one sighs,
Meeting the other's
Words with a look
That thaws suspicion.

Nineteen years now
Sharing life's table,
And not to be first
To call the meal long
We balance it thoughtfully
On the tip of the tongue,
Careful to maintain
The strict palate.

Nineteen years now
Keeping simple house,
Opening the door

To friend and stranger;
Opening the womb
Softly to let enter
The one child
With his huge hunger.

Parent

So he took her – just like that,
In a moment of sunlight;
Her haired breast heaving against his,
Her voice fierce;
Her yellow teeth bared for the love bite.

And the warm day indifferent,
Not foreseeing the loading
Of that huge womb;
The seven against Thebes, the many
Against Troy, the whole earth
A confusion of persons,
Each with his grudge
Rooted in the enormous loins
Of the first parent.

The Untamed

My garden is the wild
    Sea of the grass. Her garden
Shelters between walls.
    The tide could break in;
    I should be sorry for this.

There is peace there of a kind,
    Though not the deep peace
Of wild places. Her care
    For green life has enabled
    The weak things to grow.

Despite my first love,
    I take sometimes her hand,
Following strait paths
    Between flowers, the nostril
    Clogged with their thick scent.

The old softness of lawns
   Persuading the slow foot
Leads to defection; the silence
   Holds with its gloved hand
   The wild hawk of the mind.

But not for long, windows,
   Opening in the trees
Call the mind back
   To its true eyrie; I stoop
   Here only in play.

On the Farm

There was Dai Puw. He was no good.
They put him in the fields to dock swedes,
And took the knife from him, when he came home
At late evening with a grin
Like the slash of a knife on his face.

There was Llew Puw, and he was no good.
Every evening after the ploughing
With the big tractor he would sit in his chair,
And stare into the tangled fire garden,
Opening his slow lips like a snail.

There was Huw Puw, too. What shall I say ?
I have heard him whistling in the hedges
On and on, as though winter
Would never again leave those fields,
And all the trees were deformed.

And lastly there was the girl:
Beauty under some spell of the beast.
Her pale face was the lantern
By which they read in life's dark book
The shrill sentence: God is love.

Because

I praise you because
I envy your ability to
See these things: the blind hands
Of the aged combing sunlight
For pity; the starved fox and
The obese pet; the way the world
Digests itself and the thin flame
Scours. The youth enters
The brothel, and the girl enters
The nunnery, and a bell tolls.
Viruses invade the blood.
On the smudged empires the dust
Lies and in the libraries
Of the poets. The flowers wither
On love's grave. This is what
Life is, and on it your eye
Sets tearless, and the dark
Is dear to you as the light.

Gifts

From my father my strong heart,
My weak stomach.
From my mother the fear.

From my sad country the shame.

To my wife all I have
Saving only the love
That is not mine to give.

To my one son the hunger.

For Instance

She gave me good food;
I accepted;

Sewed my clothes, buttons;
I was smart.

She warmed my bed;
Out of it my son stepped.

She was adjudged
Beautiful. I had grown

Used to it. She is dead
Now. Is it true

I loved her? That is how
I saw things. But not she.

Exchange

She goes out.
I stay in.
Now we have been
So long together
There's no need
To share silence;
The old bed
Remains made
For two; spirits
Mate apart
From the sad flesh,
Growing thinner
On time's diet
Of bile and gall.

Blondes

They pass me with bland looks.
It is the simplicity of their lives
I ache for: prettiness and a soft heart, no problems
Not to be brought to life size
By a kiss or a smile. I see them walking
Up long streets with the accuracy of shuttles
At work, threads crossed to make a pattern
Unknown to them. A thousand curtains
Are parted to welcome home
The husbands who have overdrawn
On their blank trust, giving them children
To play with, a jingle of small change
For their pangs. The tear-laden tree
Of a poet strikes no roots in their hearts.

The Dance

She is young. Have I the right
Even to name her? Child,
It is not love I offer
Your quick limbs, your eyes;
Only the barren homage
Of an old man whom time
Crucifies. Take my hand
A moment in the dance,
Ignoring its sly pressure,
The dry rut of age,
And lead me under the boughs
Of innocence. Let me smell
My youth again in your hair.

Touching

She kept touching me,
As a woman will
Accidentally, so the response,
When given, is
A presumption.
           I retained my
Balance, letting her sway
To her cost. The lips' prose
Ticked on, regulating
Her voltage.
           Such insulation!
But necessary; their flair
For some small fun with
The current being
An injustice.
It is the man burns.

Tenancies

This is pain's landscape.
A savage agriculture is practised
Here; every farm has its
Grandfather or grandmother, gnarled hands
On the cheque-book, a long, slow
Pull on the placenta about the neck.
Old lips monopolise the talk
When a friend calls. The children listen
From the kitchen; the children march
With angry patience against the dawn.
They are waiting for someone to die
Whose name is as bitter as the soil
They handle. In clear pools
In the furrows they watch themselves grow old
To the terrible accompaniment of the song
Of the blackbird, that promises them love.

Study

The flies walk upon the roof top.
The student's eyes are too keen
To miss them. The young girls walk
In the roadway; the wind ruffles
Their skirts. The student does not look.
He sees only the flies spread their wings
And take off into the sunlight
Without sound. There is nothing to do
Now but read in his book
Of how young girls walked in the roadway
In Tyre, and how young men
Sailed off into the red west
For gold, writing dry words
To the music the girls sang.

Acting

Being unwise enough to have married her
I never knew when she was not acting.
'I love you' she would say; I heard the audiences
Sigh. 'I hate you'; I could never be sure
They were still there. She was lovely. I
Was only the looking-glass she made up in.
I husbanded the rippling meadow
Of her body. Their eyes grazed nightly upon it.

Alone now on the brittle platform
Of herself she is playing her last rôle.
It is perfect. Never in all her career
Was she so good. And yet the curtain
Has fallen. My charmer, come out from behind
It to take the applause. Look, I am clapping too.

Female

It was the other way round:
God waved his slow wand
And the creature became a woman,
Imperceptibly, retaining its body,
Nose, brow, lips, eyes,
And the face that was like a flower
On the neck's stem. The man turned to her,
Crazy with the crushed smell
Of her hair; and her eyes warned him
To keep off. And she spoke to him with the voice
Of his own conscience, and rippled there
In the shade. So he put his hands
To his face, while her forked laughter
Played on him, and his leaves fell
Silently round him, and he hung there
On himself, waiting for the God to see.

All Right

I look. You look
Away. No colour,
No ruffling of the brow's
Surface betrays
Your feeling. As though I
Were not here ; as
Though you were your own
Mirror, you arrange yourself
For the play. My eyes'
Adjectives ; the way that
I scan you ; the
Conjunction the flesh
Needs – all these
Are as nothing
To you. Serene, cool,
Motionless, no statue
Could show less
The impression of
My regard. Madam, I

Grant the artistry
Of your part. Let us
Consider it, then,
A finished performance.

I

I imagine it: Two people,
A bed; I was not
There. They dreamed of me?
No, they sought themselves
In the other, You,
They breathed. I overheard
From afar. I was nine months
Coming ... nearer, nearer;
The ugliness of the place
Daunted. I hung back
In the dark, but was cast out,
Howling. Love, they promised;
It will be love and sunlight
And joy. I took their truth
In my mouth and mumbled it
For a while, till my teeth
Grew. Ah, they cried, so you would,
Would you? I knew the cold
Of the world and preferred warmth
To freedom. I let the cord
Hang, the lawn my
Horizon. Girls came

And stared at me, but her eyes
Cowed me. Duty,
They shrilled. I saw how their lives
Frayed, and praised myself
For emotion, swallowing
My snivel.
                    Years went by;
I escaped, but never outgrew
The initial contagion.

The Casualty

I had forgotten
    the old quest for truth
        I was here for. Other cares

held me: urgencies
    of the body; a girl
        beckoned; money

had never appeared
    so ethereal; it was God's blood
        circulating in the veins

of creation; I partook
    of it like Communion, lost
        myself on my way

home, with the varying voices
    on call. Moving backward
        into a receding

future, I lost the use
        of perspective, borrowing poetry
           to buy my children

their prose. The past was a poor
        king, rendering his crown down
           for the historian. Every day

I went on with that
        metallic warfare in which
           the one casualty is love.

Marged

Was she planned?
Or is this one of life's
throw-offs? Small, taken from school
young; put to minister
to a widowed mother, who keeps
her simple, she feeds the hens,
speaks their language, is one
of them, quick, easily
frightened, with sharp
eyes, ears. When I have
been there, she keeps her perch
on my mind. I would
stroke her feathers, quieten
her, say: 'Life is
like this.' But have I
the right, who have seen plainer
women with love
in abundance, with
freedom, with money to
hand? If there is one thing
she has, it is a bird's
nature, volatile

as a bird. But even
as those among whom she
lives and moves, who look at her
with their expectant
glances, song is denied her.

Resolution

The new year brings the old resolve
to be brave, to be patient,
to suffer the betrayal of birth
without flinching, without bitter
words. The way in was hard;
the way out could be made
easy, but one must not take
it; must await decay perhaps
of the mind, certainly of the mind's
image of itself that it has
projected. The bone aches, the blood
limps like a cripple about the ruins
of one's body. Yet what are these
but the infirmities that we share
with the creatures? It is the memories
that one has, the impenitent bungler
of love, refusing for too long
to say 'yes' to that earlier gesture
of love that had brought one

forth ; it is these, as they grow
clearer with the telescoping
of the years, that constitute
for the beholder the true human pain.

Two

So you have to think
of the bone hearth where love
was kindled, of the size
of the shadows so small a flame
threw on the world's
walls, with the heavens
over them, lighting their vaster fires
to no end. He took her hand
sometimes and felt the will to be
of the poetry he could not
write. She measured him
with her moist eye for the coat
always too big. And time,
the faceless collector
of taxes, beat on their thin
door, and they opened
to him, looking beyond
him, beyond the sediment
of his myriad demands to the
bright place, where their undaunted
spirits were already walking.

Almost

Was here and was one person
and was not; knew hunger
and its excess and was too full
for words; was memory's
victim. Had he a hand
in himself? He had two
that were not his: with one
he would build, with the other
he would knock down. The earth
catered for him and he drank
blood. What was the mirror
he looked in? Over his shoulder
he saw fear, on the horizon
its likeness. A woman paused
for him on her way
nowhere and together they
made in the great darkness the
small fire that is life's decoy.

Bravo!

Oh, I know it and don't
care. I know there is nothing in me
but cells and chromosomes
waiting to beget chromosomes
and cells. You could take me to pieces
and there would be no angel hard
by, wringing its hands over
the demolition of its temple.
I accept I'm predictable,
that of the thousands of choices
open to me the computer can calculate
the one I'll make. There is a woman
I know, who is the catalyst
of my conversions, who is
a mineral to dazzle. She will
grow old and her lovers will not
pardon her for it. I have made
her songs in the laboratory
of my understanding, explosives timed
to go off in the blandness of time's face.

Synopsis

Plato offered us little
the Aristotelians did not
take back. Later Spinoza
rationalised our approach;
we were taught that love
is an intellectual mode
of our being. Yet Hume questioned
the very existence of lover
or loved. The self he left us
with was what Kant
failed to transcend or Hegel
to dissolve: that grey subject
of dread that Søren Kierkegaard
depicted crossing its thousands
of fathoms; the beast that rages
through history; that presides smiling
at the councils of the positivists.

Forest Dwellers

Men who have hardly uncurled
from their posture in the
womb. Naked. Heads bowed, not
in prayer, but in contemplation
of the earth they came from,
that suckled them on the brown
milk that builds bone not brain.

Who called them forth to walk
in the green light, their thoughts
on darkness ? Their women,
who are not Madonnas, have babes
at the breast with the wise,
time-ridden faces of the Christ
child in a painting by a Florentine

master. The warriors prepare poison
with love's care for the Sebastians
of their arrows. They have no
God, but follow the contradictions
of a ritual that says
life must die that life
may go on. They wear flowers in their hair.

He and She

When he came in, she was there.
When she looked at him,
he smiled. There were lights
in time's wave breaking
on an eternal shore.

Seated at table –
no need for the fracture
of the room's silence; noiselessly
they conversed. Thoughts mingling
were lit up, gold
particles in the mind's stream.

Were there currents between them?
Why, when he thought darkly,
would the nerves play
at her lips' brim? What was the heart's depth?
There were fathoms in her,
too, and sometimes he crossed
them and landed and was not repulsed.

Siân

Can one make love
to a kitten? Siân,
purr for me; jump
into my lap; knead
me. Shine your claws
in my smile. Your talk is a bell
fastened with ribbon
about your throat. My hand
thrills to the electricity
of your fur. So small
you are, I cradle
you on my arm, wearing
you at my breast-bone. Tune
your pulses to mine.
I know the slits in your eyes
are not to be peeped
through; evidence rather
that you can find your way
through the thick of the darkness
that all too often manages
to invest my heart.

Fugue for Ann Griffiths

In which period
    do you get lost?
The roads lead
    under a twentieth century
sky to the peace
    of the nineteenth. There it is,
as she left it,
    too small to be chrysalis
of that clenched soul.
    Under the eaves the martins
continue her singing.
    Down this path she set off
for the earlier dancing
    of the body; but under the myrtle
the Bridegroom was waiting
    for her on her way home.

To put it differently
yet the same, listen,
friend:
      A nineteenth century
               calm;

that is, a countryside
          not fenced in
by cables and pylons,
but open to thought to blow in
          from as near as may be
to the truth.
                    There were evenings
she would break it. See her
          at the dance, round
and round, hand
          in hand, weaving
invisible threads. When
you are young ... But
          there was One
with his eye on her;
          she saw him stand
under the branches.
                    History insists
on a marriage, but the husband was as cuckolded
as Joseph.
          Listen again:

To the knocker at the door:
'Miss Thomas has gone dancing.'

To the caller in time:
'The mistress is sitting the dance

out with God at her side.'
To the traveller up learning's

slope: 'She is ahead of you on her knees.
She who had decomposed

is composed again in her hymns.
The dust settles on the Welsh language,

but is blown away in great gusts
week by week in chapel after chapel.'

Is there a scholarship that grows
naturally as the lichen? How
did she, a daughter of the land, come
by her learning? You have seen
her face, figure-head of a ship
outward bound? But she was not
alone; a trinity of persons
saw to it she kept on course
like one apprenticed since early
days to the difficulty of navigation
in rough seas. She described her turbulence
to her confessor, who was the more
astonished at the fathoms
of anguish over which she had
attained to the calmness of her harbours.

There are other pilgrimages
    to make beside Jerusalem, Rome ;
beside the one into the no-man's-
    land beyond the microscope's carry.

    If you came in winter,
        you would find the tree
    with your belief still crucified
        upon it, that for her at all

    times was in blossom, the resurrection
        of one that had come seminally
    down to raise the deciduous human
        body to the condition of his body.

Hostilities were other peoples'.
Though a prisoner of the Lord
she was taken without fighting.

That was in the peace before
the wars that were to end
war. If there was a campaign

for her countrymen, it was one
against sin. Musically
they were conscripted to proclaim

Sunday after Sunday the year
round they were on God's side. England
meanwhile detected its enemies
from afar. These made friends
out in the fields because
of its halo with the ancestral scarecrow.

Has she waited all these years
for me to forget myself
and do her homage? I begin
now: Ann Thomas, Ann Griffiths,
one of a thousand Anns chosen
to confound your parentage
with your culture – I know
Powys, the leafy backwaters
it is easy for the spirit to forget
its destiny in and put on soil
for its crown. You walked solitary
there and were not tempted,
or took your temptation as calling
to see Christ rising in April
out of that same soil and clothing
his nakedness like a tree. Your similes
were agricultural and profound.
As winter is forgiven by spring's
blossom, so defoliated man,
thrusting his sick hand in the earth's

side is redeemed by conviction.
Ann, dear, what can our scholarship
do but wander like Efyrnwy
your grass library, wondering at the absence
of all volumes but one ? The question
teases us like the undying
echo of an Amen high up
in the cumulus rafters over Dolanog.

The theologians disagree
on their priorities. For her
the centuries' rhetoric contracted
to the three-letter word. What was sin
but the felix culpa enabling
a daughter of the soil to move
in divine circles ? This was before
the bomb, before the annihilation
of six million Jews. It appears now
the confession of a child before
an upholstered knee ; her achievement
the sensitising of the Welsh
conscience to the English rebuke.
The contemporary miracle is the feeding
of the multitude on the sublime
mushroom, while the Jesus,
who was her lover, is a face
gathering moss on the gable

of a defunct chapel, a myth shifting
its place to the wrong end
of the spectrum under the Doppler
effect of the recession of our belief.

Three pilgrimages to Bardsey
equalling one to Rome – How close
need a shrine be to be too far
for the traveller of today who is in
a hurry? Spare an hour or two
for Dolanog – no stone cross,
no Holy Father. What question
has the country to ask, looking as if
nothing has happened since the earth
cooled? And what is your question?
She was young and was taken.
If one asked you: 'Are you glad
to have been born?' would you let
the positivist reply for you
by putting your car in gear, or watch
the exuberance of nature in a lost
village, that is life saying Amen
to itself? Here for a few years
the spirit sang on a bone bough
at eternity's window, the flesh trembling
at the splendour of a forgiveness
too impossible to believe in, yet believing.

Are the Amens over? Ann (Gymraeg)
you have gone now but left us with the question
that has a child's simplicity and a child's depth:
Does the one who called to you,

when the tree was green, call us
also, if with changed voice,
now the leaves have fallen and the boughs
are of plastic, to the same thing?

She listened to him.
We listen to her.
She was in time
chosen. We but infer
from the union of time
with space the possibility
of survival. She who was born
first must be overtaken
by our tomorrow.
So with wings pinned
and fuel rationed,
let us put on speed
to remain still
through the dark hours
in which prayer gathers
on the brow like dew,
where at dawn the footprints

of one who invisibly
but so close passed
discover a direction.

A Marriage

We met
        under a shower
of bird-notes.
        Fifty years passed,
love's moment
        in a world in
servitude to time.
        She was young;
I kissed with my eyes
        closed and opened
them on her wrinkles.
        'Come,' said death,
choosing her as his
        partner for
the last dance. And she,
        who in life
had done everything
        with a bird's grace,
opened her bill now
        for the shedding
of one sigh no
        heavier than a feather.

A Note on R. S. Thomas

R. S. Thomas is widely recognised as one of the finest poets writing in English in the second half of the twentieth century. From his first book, *The Stones of the Field* (1946), through more than twenty other collections leading to his acclaimed *Collected Poems 1945–1990*, he has been a major figure in the landscape of contemporary poetry. His is a strongly individual voice: he is the leading Christian poet of our time and a spokesman for people and cultures resisting the destruction of traditional and religious values.

R. S. Thomas was born in Cardiff in 1913, and brought up in Liverpool and Holyhead. He was a priest in the Church of Wales until his retirement in 1978. He lives in Gwynedd. He won the Heinemann Award in 1955, the Queen's Medal for poetry in 1964 and the Cholmondeley Award in 1978. He has received three Welsh Arts Council Literature Awards. His autobiography *Neb* was published in Welsh in 1985; it will be published, with other autobiographical writings, in English in 1996. His most recent book of poems is *No Truce With The Furies* (1995). He has been nominated for the Nobel Prize for Literature for 1996.

Other titles in this series

ANDREW MARVELL *To His Coy Mistress*

JOHN MILTON *Paradise Lost*

WILFRED OWEN *The Pity of War*

PALGRAVE *Golden Treasury of Love Poems*

EDGAR ALLAN POE *The Raven*

ALEXANDER POPE *The Rape of the Lock*

CHRISTINA ROSSETTI *Goblin Market*

SIR WALTER SCOTT *Lochinvar*

WILLIAM SHAKESPEARE *Love Sonnets*

PERCY BYSSHE SHELLEY *To a Skylark*

EDMUND SPENSER *The Fairy Queen*

ALFRED, LORD TENNYSON *The Lady of Shalott*

DYLAN THOMAS *Fern Hill*

EDWARD THOMAS *There Was a Time*

R. S. THOMAS *Love Poems*

FRANCIS THOMPSON *The Hound of Heaven*

WALT WHITMAN *I Sing the Body Electric*

WILLIAM WORDSWORTH *Intimations of Immortality*

W. B. YEATS *Sailing to Byzantium*